HISTORIC AMERICAN BATTLES for KIDS

WWI, WWII, Vietnam, Desert Storm & More!

20TH CENTURY EDITION

A GUIDE TO THE 1900'S BATTLES
THAT FORGED A NATION

ETHAN CARTER

This book is a work of nonfiction intended to educate and entertain young readers. All facts have been presented in a simplified, age-appropriate way. Every effort has been made to ensure accuracy at the time of publication.

Author: Ethan Carter

Publisher: Intel-Excellence

First Edition, September 2025

ISBN: 978-1-969899-01-0

Printed in USA

For permissions, visit: www.intel-excellence.com

TABLE OF CONTENTS

INTRODUCTION

Okay, brave reader.

Are you ready for a book so full of action, adventure, and history that your socks might just fly off? Good! Because you're about to dive into the wildest, and most important moments in American battle history from the 1900s!

This isn't just any history book. Think of it as a time machine powered by curiosity! We're going to blast back through the 20th Century to see how American soldiers, sailors, pilots, and even Marines became heroes.

But wait—history doesn't have to be dusty and boring! We're going to zoom in on the biggest, boldest fights where things got seriously intense. So, let's check the date on our time machine and get ready to go!

Hold on tight! The 20th Century was a busy time for America, with soldiers fighting in huge conflicts all over the world. Our book zooms in on some of the most famous moments.

We've got battles from:

World War I (The Great War)

World War II (The war that was even greater... and harder!)

The Korean War

The Vietnam War

And even the Gulf War!

Imagine a video game where every level is a real historical event. This book is the ultimate cheat sheet!

Speaking of cheats... Why did the U.S. Marine ask for a fork and knife in the trenches?

...Because he heard the other side was serving the Battle of Hamburger Hill! (Okay, that battle isn't actually in our book, but it sounds tasty, right?)

In this book, you'll meet brave people in impossible situations.

Take a look at 1950, during the Korean War. We're going to see the incredible Battle of Inchon! Imagine trying to sneak a giant landing right behind enemy lines, where the tides are so tricky it was a "500-to-1 shot!" That's like trying to land a huge boat in a bathtub... only way more important!

Then there's the famous Attack on Pearl Harbor in 1941. This surprise event changed the course of World War II and woke up a "sleeping giant"—the American military! This event taught America one thing: always check your watch!

We'll also look at one of the scariest retreats ever, the Battle of Chosin Reservoir in 1950, where Marines battled the cold and the enemy, proving just how tough they were! Seriously, those Marines were so tough, the snow complained they were too cold!

Get ready to see the battles that were all about fighting to the very end!

In 1945, American forces fought the intense Battle of Iwo Jima and the bloody Battle of Okinawa. These were islands protected by determined enemy defenders. It took every ounce of courage to win those.

Why did the Marines on Iwo Jima bring a ladder?

...To get a better view when they raised the flag! (A moment so famous, it's printed on a million posters!)

You'll also get a look at more modern action, like in 1991, during the first Gulf War. We'll see two major tank clashes: the Battle of 73 Easting and the Battle of Khafji. These were where American tanks showed the world they were the fastest and the fiercest! It was like a giant race, but with exploding tanks instead of trophies!

And let's not forget the Marines who landed in Cuba in 1961 during the disastrous Bay of Pigs operation. It was a tough lesson learned about covert ops!

This book is your ticket to a world of real-life heroes, incredible strategy, and the unforgettable moments that shaped the United States.

It's an adventure that is:

Fun (Because history is awesome!)

Factual (Because it all really happened!)

Full of Fights (The kind you only read about!)

So, go ahead! Turn the page, buckle up your brain-helmet, and prepare for a journey into the past. Get ready for an adventure that proves why the history of American battles is exciting, important, and absolutely unforgettable!

Let the adventures begin!

1918
BATTLE OF BELLEAU WOOD

Think of the world like a giant game of Capture the Flag that had been going on since 1914. It was muddy, it was messy, and everyone was exhausted. The two sides—the Allies (that's the good guys, including France and Britain) and the Central Powers (mainly Germany)—were stuck in trenches, which are basically long, stinky ditches. It was awful!

But in 1918, the German Army decided they had enough of being stuck in the mud. They launched a huge, desperate attack called the Spring Offensive. Their target? Paris! The beautiful, bustling capital of France! If they captured Paris, the war was over, and they won.

So, the German forces pushed and pushed, rolling closer to the capital every day. The French and British soldiers defending the area were worn out and stretched thin. They needed a miracle. They needed heroes.

And guess who arrived?

Yep! In a dramatic entrance, the fresh, enthusiastic, and super-tough American forces—known as the American Expeditionary Forces (AEF), led by a general named John J. Pershing—were finally streaming into France. These American troops were young, they were ready, and they were about to get their first huge test! It was like calling up the backup squad, and the backup squad was really good at football!

A Forest Named "Belleau"

The German troops were sweeping through the countryside in early June 1918. They needed to secure a specific area so they could keep moving quickly toward Paris. This area included a small, but very important, piece of land called Belleau Wood.

Now, "Belleau Wood" sounds fancy and peaceful, doesn't it? That's because, in French, "Belleau" means "beautiful water." It used to be a lovely hunting forest with trees, rocks, and a clear stream.

But by 1918, this forest was anything but beautiful. The Germans had turned it into a deadly fortress! They packed every thicket and patch of trees with machine guns. These weren't little BB guns; these were giant, fast-firing weapons that could cut down soldiers like a lawnmower cuts grass.

Why was this small forest so important? Because it sat right next to a key road that led straight to Paris, which was only about fifty miles away! It was the ultimate traffic jam, and the Germans were the angry drivers blocking the highway!

When the exhausted French troops finally fell back to the nearby roads, they spotted the arriving Americans—specifically, the brave fighting men of the U.S. Army's 2nd Division, which included the legendary 4th Marine Brigade.

The French commander saw the German advance and quickly told the American officers to retreat, to fall back, to run away to a safer place.

And that brings us to the most famous, fire-up-your-cheerleader-squad moment of the whole battle...

The Best "NO!" in History

Imagine someone telling you to run away from a big bully, but you know you're strong enough to stand your ground. That's exactly what happened.

A Marine captain named Lloyd Williams was told by the French officer: "You must retreat! The situation is terrible!"

And Captain Williams, a man who clearly hadn't received the memo about politely running away, stood there, looked the French officer right in the eye, and delivered a line that is now legendary. He said:

"Retreat, hell! We just got here!"

How awesome is that?! It was the American way of saying, "We didn't travel all this way across the ocean just to run home! Time to fight!"

This moment was a huge shot of energy for the tired Allies. They saw the fresh, confident Americans planting their feet and refusing to budge. The American forces began setting up their defenses, ready for the German wave to crash right into them.

The battle officially started on June 6, 1918, and it was anything but pretty. The German troops, confident from their easy advance against the retreating French, thought taking on the Americans would be a breeze.

But they were wrong. Boy, were they wrong.

The Birth of the Devil Dogs!

The fighting in Belleau Wood was brutal. The Marines didn't fight neatly in lines; they had to crawl and jump through thick trees, rocky terrain, and tall wheat fields, trying to find and destroy machine gun nests. It was like playing a deadly game of hide-and-seek where the "seekers" had machine guns!

The Americans were using a special trick called fire and maneuver, where some guys would shoot while others moved forward. It was slow, agonizing work, and the Germans were waiting for them everywhere.

The Americans, especially the Marines, fought with a ferocity the German soldiers had never seen. They charged through the machine gun fire, refusing to surrender or retreat. Many of them ran so fast and fought so fiercely that the shocked Germans started calling them a special name.

The nickname they gave the Marines was Teufelshunde, which means "Devil Dogs!"

Joke Time! Why did the Germans call them Devil Dogs?

...Because they always growled when they had to share a tin of cold beans! (Actually, it was because they were relentless and fierce fighters, but the bean joke is funnier.)

The battle raged for three grueling weeks! Every tree, every rock, and every piece of ground was fought for. The Marines ran out of supplies, they ran out of water, but they never ran out of fight.

They kept attacking, day after day, until they had cleared the Germans out of the woods. The constant counter-attacks and determination finally broke the German morale. The enemy offensive, the one that threatened to win the war, was officially stopped at this tiny, once-beautiful forest.

Mission Accomplished: The Woods Are Ours!

Finally, on June 26, 1918, after twenty days of non-stop combat, the Marines were able to secure the last remaining German positions. The forest belonged to the United States and the Allies.

The commanding officer sent a simple, powerful message back to headquarters to confirm the great victory. He wrote:

"Woods now U.S. Marine Corps entirely."

This wasn't just the end of a battle; it was the end of the German offensive that was supposed to win them the war! The sheer determination shown by the Americans proved to the world that they were a powerful and critical new force. It also cemented the reputation of the US Marines as some of the toughest fighters on the planet—a legacy they still hold today!

Because of this battle, the Marines earned the name Teufelshunde, which they wear proudly! They learned that day how to fight bravely in the mud, through the trees, and against impossible odds.

It's a fantastic story of courage, and it's just one of the many amazing moments we'll explore in the history of American battles! Now, turn the page and let's jump ahead to the next big conflict!

Quiz Time

1. What was the main goal of the massive German 'Spring Offensive' in 1918?

   a) To capture the capital city of Paris and win the war.
   b) To stop the French and British from making chocolate cake.
   c) To build a brand new trench system near the ocean.
   d) To find Captain Lloyd Williams and ask him to surrender.

2. The Marines were sent to defend Belleau Wood. What does 'Belleau' mean in French?

   a) Beautiful Water
   b) Bloody Hill
   c) Machine Gun Nest
   d) Angry Bear

3. What famous response did Captain Lloyd Williams give when asked to retreat?

   a) "Can we stop for cold beans first?"
   b) "Wait for backup, then we'll think about it!"
   c) "Please leave a message after the beep."
   d) "Retreat, hell! We just got here!"

4. The American forces that rushed to the defense of the area were called the AEF. What does AEF stand for?

   a) Armored Elite Force
   b) Alliance of European Friends
   c) Awesome Expeditionary Fighters
   d) American Expeditionary Forces

1941
ATTACK ON PEARL HARBOR

Let's leave the cold, muddy trenches of World War I behind and zoom our time machine forward a few years to 1941. We're traveling all the way to the beautiful, sunny islands of Hawaii!

In the years before 1941, things were getting really wild and scary in the world. World War II had already started in Europe in 1939. Germany, led by the serious bad guy Adolf Hitler, was marching all over Europe, and Germany's ally,

Japan, was doing the same thing across the huge Pacific Ocean.

Now, America, led by President Franklin D. Roosevelt (FDR), really, really wanted to stay out of the war. But America had built up a huge, powerful Navy, especially its Pacific Fleet, and parked most of those mighty ships in one place: Pearl Harbor, on the island of Oahu.

Why did Japan see this as a problem? Because Japan wanted to become the biggest, baddest empire in the Pacific. To do that, they needed resources like oil and rubber, which meant taking over islands held by America and its friends. And standing right in their way was that giant American fleet at Pearl Harbor. It was like Japan wanted to steal all the cookies, but America had the biggest, scariest watchdog sitting right next to the cookie jar!

The Japanese commanders knew that if they could knock out the American Navy quickly and completely, they'd have months, maybe even a whole year, to take all the islands they wanted before America could build a new fleet. They decided on a sneaky plan: a massive, secret surprise attack!

The Quiet Before the Thunder

Let's imagine Pearl Harbor on Sunday, December 7, 1941.

It was a perfect tropical morning. The water was blue, the palm trees were swaying, and most of the sailors and soldiers stationed there were taking it easy. Many were sleeping late, eating breakfast, or getting ready for church. No one expected trouble. In fact, many were worried about a different kind of Sunday surprise.

The US military had set up some radar stations (giant screens that check for planes), and they even saw a massive group of aircraft heading toward them. But the officer who saw the blips thought it was just a group of American planes flying in from California. Mistake! It was actually the first wave of over 350 Japanese fighter planes and bombers!

Chaos Arrives in Waves

At precisely 7:55 a.m., the skies filled with a noise like a thousand angry hornets! The Japanese attack began. It was a terrifying, violent shock.

The planes swooped down, dropping bombs and torpedoes on the anchored ships. The torpedoes—long, underwater missiles—were specially designed to run in the shallow waters of the harbor.

The biggest targets were the enormous battleships. In just a few minutes, the famous battleship USS Arizona was hit by a huge bomb that went through its deck and exploded its forward ammunition magazine.

The explosion was catastrophic and instant. The ship sank in minutes, and sadly, over 1,177 crew members were killed on board. The hull of the USS Arizona still rests at the bottom of the harbor today, serving as a memorial to the brave men lost that morning.

Chaos erupted everywhere:

Sailors scrambled out of beds and raced to their battle stations.

The sky was thick with smoke and anti-aircraft fire (that's when the ships and ground crews shot back at the planes).

Bombs were hitting airfields, destroying American planes before they could even get off the ground to fight back!

Heroes Fight Back

Even in the complete chaos and total surprise, true American heroism shone through.

There wasn't time for a plan, just time for bravery. Every sailor and soldier grabbed whatever weapon they could find and fought back.

One incredible hero was a young Black sailor named Doris "Dorie" Miller. Dorie was a cook—yes, a cook!—on the battleship USS West Virginia. His job wasn't to fight; it was to serve food. But when the battle started, he rushed to a machine gun, which he had never even been trained to fire, and started shooting at the incoming Japanese aircraft! He shot down several planes and helped rescue his wounded captain, becoming one of the first American heroes of World War II.

Another amazing story is of the few American pilots who did manage to get their planes in the air. Flying into the teeth of the enemy attack, these brave few pilots were like mosquitoes fighting a swarm of angry bees—but they fought with everything they had, defending their homeland.

The whole attack lasted about two hours, but the damage was unbelievable. Over 2,400 Americans were killed, and 18 ships were sunk or heavily damaged.

The Sleeping Giant Awakens

The day after the attack, President FDR stood before the American Congress and made one of the most famous speeches in American history. He called December 7, 1941, "A date which will live in infamy."

The attack did not achieve Japan's main goal. They sank ships, but the most important targets—America's aircraft carriers—were out at sea that morning and untouched. They also failed to destroy the vital fuel depots and repair shops at Pearl Harbor.

Most importantly, the attack did exactly what Japan hoped to avoid: it woke up the "sleeping giant" of the United States. Before Pearl Harbor, Americans were divided about joining the war. Afterward, the entire country was united and angry, determined to fight back and win.

America immediately declared war on Japan, and days later, Germany and Italy declared war on the US. The United States was fully in World War II, and the fight was officially on, across two huge oceans!

The Attack on Pearl Harbor remains a powerful reminder of courage in the face of sudden tragedy. It was a dark day, but it was the moment America became a full and unstoppable force on the world stage.

Now, let's turn the page and see how America took the fight to the enemy in the Pacific and Europe!

Quiz Time

1. **What was the exact date of the surprise attack on Pearl Harbor?**

    a) November 7, 1941
    b) December 7, 1941
    c) January 11, 1942
    d) February 36, 1943

2. **Who was the hero sailor on the USS West Virginia who jumped onto a machine gun he wasn't trained for?**

    a) Franklin D. Roosevelt
    b) Doris 'Dorie' Miller
    c) Captain Lloyd Williams
    d) Chester Nimitz

3. **The Japanese achieved a lot of damage, but they failed to hit what most important target, which helped the US fight back later in the war?**

    a) The entire fleet of small fishing boats
    b) The sailors' breakfast eggs
    c) America's mighty aircraft carriers
    d) The giant radar screens

4. **What nickname did the United States get after the attack?**

    a) The Tidy Gardener
    b) The Sleeping Giant
    c) The Quiet Mouse
    d) The Angry Hornet

1944 BATTLE OF THE BULGE

Hello, history explorers! We're jumping ahead to the very end of 1944. By this time, the Allies (that's America, Britain, France, and their friends) had kicked the German army out of France and were pushing hard towards Germany itself. Everyone thought the war in Europe would be over by Christmas! But the German leader, Adolf Hitler, had one last, crazy, secret plan.

Imagine you've been running a marathon for weeks, and you're exhausted. You think you're close to the finish line, so you relax a little and slow your pace. That's exactly how the American forces felt in the Ardennes Forest of Belgium. This area was thick with trees, rough hills, and, most importantly, it was quiet. The generals thought it was too difficult for the German army to attack, so they put their tired troops there for a rest and stationed mostly new, inexperienced American soldiers to guard the line.

The weather matched the mood: freezing cold, cloudy, and snowy. The low clouds meant the mighty American Air Force, which usually blasted the Germans with bombs, couldn't even fly!

Joke Time! Why did the American soldiers in the Ardennes start telling so many jokes?

...Because they were trying to break the ice! (And they needed something to keep their minds off the cold!)

This was exactly what Hitler was waiting for.

Hitler's Desperate Dice Roll

Hitler knew his army was running out of gas (literally, they were low on fuel!) and troops. So, he planned one massive, final, all-or-nothing punch: a huge surprise attack through the snowy Ardennes.

His goal was gigantic and desperate:

Smash through the thin American lines in the Ardennes.

Race 60 miles to the coast and capture the huge supply port of Antwerp, Belgium.

Split the Allied armies (separating the British from the Americans).

Hitler hoped if he could do this, the Allies would panic and agree to a peace treaty, letting him off the hook! It was the riskiest, most reckless move of the war, and the Germans called it Operation Watch on the Rhine.

On December 16, 1944, just before dawn, the Germans launched their attack.

The Attack Creates the "Bulge"

It was a total shock. More than 200,000 German troops and nearly 1,000 tanks slammed into the American lines.

The German attack worked so well and pushed the American lines back so far and so quickly that, when military strategists looked at the map, the front line looked like a giant, dangerous bulge sticking out into the Allied territory. That's how the battle got its famous name: The Battle of the Bulge!

In many places, the American soldiers, who were completely surprised and outgunned, were overwhelmed. They fought fiercely, but some units were forced to retreat, and many soldiers were captured.

But here's the most important part: even though the German army was moving fast, many small American units, often surrounded and freezing, refused to run. They held key roads, bridges, and towns, acting like giant speed bumps that kept slowing the powerful German tanks down. Every hour they held out was an hour lost for Hitler.

Historical Fact: One of the most terrifying things about this battle was the German plan to use soldiers in captured American uniforms to sneak behind the lines and cause chaos. This meant American soldiers had to constantly quiz each other on random American facts, like who won the World Series or what city was the capital!

The Siege of Bastogne: The Best Nuts Joke Ever

The most critical small town that needed holding was Bastogne, an important hub where seven major roads met. If the Germans captured it, their tanks could race through easily and speed toward Antwerp.

Luckily, Bastogne was defended by the legendary 101st Airborne Division (paratroopers who usually jumped out of planes) and the 10th Armored Division. On December 20, the Germans completely surrounded the town. The Americans were trapped, freezing, and running low on food, medicine, and ammo.

The German commander sent a formal demand for the American commander to surrender. The commander of the 101st Airborne, Brigadier General Anthony C. McAuliffe, read the German note. He wasn't scared, just annoyed.

After thinking for a moment, he wrote a one-word reply, which became the most famous, defiant answer of the entire war:

"NUTS!"

Joke Time! Why did General McAuliffe respond with "NUTS!"?

...Because he was a general, not a kernel, and he wasn't about to crack under pressure! (Plus, it was a perfectly clear way to tell the Germans to go jump in a frozen lake!)

This one word told the Germans everything they needed to know: the Americans were not giving up Bastogne!

Patton's Race and the Weather Switch

While the 101st Airborne was holding Bastogne, a hero named General George S. Patton Jr. was making history. Patton, a general known for his fiery speeches, pearl-handled pistols, and love of speed, was hundreds of miles away, fighting in France.

When the attack started, Patton immediately knew he had to turn his massive Third Army around and drive north through the snow to rescue Bastogne. In an impossible feat of logistics and speed, Patton managed to turn his entire army (thousands of vehicles and men) 90 degrees and launch a powerful counter-attack in just three days! Military experts say that was the fastest large-scale movement in the history of mechanized warfare.

But Patton needed help. The German attack had worked so well because the clouds kept the Allied airplanes grounded.

Patton, a man who believed in prayer as much as tank tracks, famously asked the military chaplain for a prayer to clear the weather. And guess what? On December 23, just three days before Christmas, the clouds miraculously cleared!

The Allied Air Force instantly took off, flooding the skies with planes. They began bombing the now-exposed German supply lines and dropping vital supplies (including fresh medical kits and, yes, ammo!) to the surrounded troops in Bastogne.

With Patton attacking from the south and the Air Force attacking from above, the Bulge began to shrink.

Victory and Legacy

By the middle of January 1945, the American and Allied forces had pushed the Germans all the way back to their starting lines. The attack failed completely. Hitler's last, desperate punch had been blocked and broken.

The Battle of the Bulge was the largest and bloodiest single battle fought by the United States Army in World War II. It showed the world that even when surprised and surrounded in the worst conditions imaginable, the American soldier would never quit.

It cost Hitler his last reserves of men, tanks, and, most importantly, fuel. After this colossal failure, Germany had nothing left for a major attack. The road to final Allied victory in Europe was now wide open.

Now that we've seen the surprise attack that started the end, let's travel to the Pacific and see another brutal challenge waiting for the Marines!

Quiz Time

1. The Battle of the Bulge got its name because the German attack caused what shape on the military maps?

    a) A perfect circle, like a donut
    b) A giant, dangerous outward curve, or 'bulge'
    c) A straight, neat line across Belgium
    d) A letter 'S' for surprise

2. What one-word answer did General McAuliffe give the Germans when they demanded his surrender?

    a) Surrender!
    b) Impossible!
    c) Nuts!
    d) Christmas!

3. What critical target was Hitler desperately trying to reach and capture with this surprise attack?

    a) The massive supply port of Antwerp, Belgium
    b) The frozen lake where the soldiers were breaking the ice
    c) Paris, France, for the second time
    d) The American Air Force headquarters

4. What heroic general raced his entire Third Army northward in just three days to relieve the troops surrounded at Bastogne?

    a) Brigadier General Anthony C. McAuliffe
    b) General George S. Patton Jr.
    c) Adolf Hitler
    d) General Eisenhower

1945 BATTLE OF IWO JIMA

We've jumped ahead again, this time to 1945, the final year of World War II.

Remember how the United States was fighting two huge wars at once? We saw how the amazing Allied forces broke Hitler's last big surprise, the Battle of the Bulge, in Europe. Now, we turn all our attention to the Pacific Ocean, where the war against Japan was getting tougher and tougher.

The American strategy was called "Island Hopping." It was exactly what it sounds like: capturing one island, building a base there, and then hopping to the next island closer to Japan. Every island we hopped to was stronger, and the resistance was fiercer.

In February 1945, there was one tiny island—only eight square miles, which is about the size of a giant park—that sat in the middle of the ocean. It was a smelly, ugly volcanic rock, but it was absolutely vital. This island was called Iwo Jima. (Say it with me: EE-wo JEE-muh).

The name Iwo Jima actually means "Sulphur Island" because of all the volcanic gases and stinky smells coming out of it.

Joke Time! Why was the island of Iwo Jima the unluckiest place in the Pacific?

...Because it had a terrible atmosphere! (Get it? Sulphur smells and the fierce fighting!)

But why was this smelly little island so important?

The Airfield Game Changer

Iwo Jima was like a crucial pit stop in a race. It sat right in the middle of the long journey between the Mariana Islands (where the giant American B-29 Superfortress bombers took off) and Japan.

These B-29 bombers were flying nine hours just to reach Japan, drop their bombs, and then fly nine hours back. That's eighteen hours! If a bomber was damaged by enemy fire, it had nowhere safe to land, and the crew had to crash into the ocean.

Iwo Jima had two airfields that the Japanese were using, and if the Americans could capture them, it would change everything:

B-29s could land safely if they were damaged, saving thousands of American pilots' lives.

Smaller fighter planes could take off from Iwo Jima and fly all the way to Japan to protect the big B-29 bombers.

For the Americans, taking Iwo Jima was not just about winning a battle; it was about saving the lives of the Air Force crews who were trying to finish the war.

The Fortress Under the Volcano

The Japanese knew exactly why Iwo Jima was important, and they planned a defense unlike anything the Americans had ever seen. The Japanese commander, General Tadamichi Kuribayashi, was brilliant and determined. He knew he couldn't win the island back, but he could make taking it cost so many lives that America might give up the war.

Instead of building traditional defenses on the beaches (which would get blown up by the US Navy), he used the island's unique volcanic features.

Iwo Jima was dominated by a huge, dormant volcano on its southern tip called Mount Suribachi. Kuribayashi decided to turn the entire island, including the volcano, into a giant underground bunker.

Tunnels and Caves: His soldiers dug over eleven miles of crisscrossing tunnels, bunkers, and caves deep into the rock. It was a secret city underground!

Hidden Firepower: The Japanese placed machine guns and cannons inside these caves, with tiny slits to shoot out of. From the outside, the Marines would see nothing but rock and black sand.

No Retreat: Kuribayashi strictly ordered his soldiers: no glorious suicide charges. They were to stay hidden, fight to the death, and take as many Marines with them as possible.

The American Navy and Air Force bombed Iwo Jima for 74 straight days before the invasion, thinking they had destroyed everything. They were wrong. General Kuribayashi and his 21,000 defenders were just waiting, hidden deep below the surface.

Historical Context: Iwo Jima was so heavily fortified that Kuribayashi's plan was studied by military experts for decades afterward. He used the geography of the island—the volcano and the soft volcanic ash—to protect his troops perfectly.

Landing on the Black Sand

The official start of the invasion, or "D-Day" for Iwo Jima, was February 19, 1945.

As the sun rose, the United States Marines—America's toughest fighters—piled into landing boats. More than 70,000 Marines were about to hit the beaches, which were named Green, Red, Yellow, and Blue.

The moment the Marines jumped off the boats, they faced two horrible facts:

The Sand: The beaches weren't normal sand. They were made of thick, black volcanic ash, like super-heavy, sticky wet cement. Every step the Marines took made them sink up to their ankles, sometimes knees! They struggled to carry their heavy packs, and their trucks and jeeps got instantly stuck. It was a messy, slow slog, like walking through wet oatmeal!

The Silence: For the first hour, there was almost no resistance. The Marines thought the bombing had worked! But the silence was a cruel trick. General Kuribayashi was waiting until the beaches were full of Marines, tanks, and supplies.

When the beaches were jammed with struggling men and stuck machines, the island erupted. Machine guns fired from invisible slits in the volcano, cannons shot out from the high ground, and the Japanese began firing mortars and rockets. The beaches instantly turned into a nightmare.

Joke Time! Why did the Marine commander yell at his soldier for carrying a spoon?

...Because he told him, "This isn't a retreat, and we aren't having any more wet oatmeal!"

The Marines were pinned down by fire coming from places they couldn't even see, and the thick, soft sand meant they couldn't even dig foxholes (small defensive holes) for protection. They had to fight forward, meter by painful meter.

The Climb to Suribachi

The main goal on the first day was to isolate Mount Suribachi, the 550-foot volcano dominating the southern end of the island. It was like climbing a fortress, where every rock and hole could hide a sniper.

The fighting was unlike anything the Marines had ever faced. It wasn't about big charges; it was about small groups of men using a tactic called Fire and Maneuver (like we saw at Belleau Wood) to slowly eliminate each hidden position, one at a time. The Marines had to use flamethrowers and grenades to clear the deep, dark caves, knowing that the enemy would never surrender.

The Marines who fought here were incredible. They fought day and night, barely sleeping, always pushing up the slippery slopes of the volcano.

Finally, on the morning of February 23, 1945, four days after the invasion began, a patrol reached the summit of Mount Suribachi.

The Most Famous Photo in History

When the first patrol reached the top of the volcano, they immediately tied a small American flag to a pipe they found lying nearby and raised it. It was a tiny flag, but when the Marines and sailors on the beaches saw it flying from the peak, a massive cheer went up across the entire island and the ships at sea! It was a huge moment of hope and victory.

But that small flag was hard to see from far away. A short time later, the leaders decided to replace it with a much larger, easier-to-see flag.

A team of six Marines was gathered to raise this second, larger flag. As they strained and pushed the heavy metal pipe into the ground, raising the Stars and Stripes high above the volcano, an Associated Press photographer named Joe Rosenthal snapped a photo.

The Result: That photograph—of the six tired, tough Marines raising the flag—became the most famous and powerful image of World War II. It was a picture of courage, teamwork, and the stubborn American will to win. It immediately inspired everyone back home and helped the nation understand the price being paid in the Pacific.

The Cost and the Legacy

But the fight wasn't over. While the flag was flying on Suribachi, the rest of the island still had to be captured.

General Kuribayashi's main forces were still hidden in the tunnels and caves on the northern end of Iwo Jima.

The battle raged for another grueling 32 days, not ending until March 26, 1945.

The cost of this small island was staggering:

Over 6,800 American Marines and sailors were killed (a huge number for such a tiny piece of land).

Nearly 20,000 Americans were wounded.

Of the 21,000 Japanese defenders, only about 1,000 were captured; the rest fought exactly as General Kuribayashi had ordered.

The battle was terrible, but it was not fought in vain. Within a few weeks of its capture, Iwo Jima's airfields were fully operational. Over the rest of the war, more than 2,200 damaged B-29 bombers made emergency landings on Iwo Jima, saving the lives of almost 25,000 airmen.

The Battle of Iwo Jima proved the famous words of Admiral Chester Nimitz, who said that on Iwo Jima, "Uncommon valor was a common virtue." It means that in that place, extraordinary courage was ordinary—every soldier was a hero.

It was one of the final steps before the final defeat of Japan, and the flag raised on that black volcanic sand remains the ultimate symbol of the Pacific war hero.

Quiz Time

1. Why was the tiny island of Iwo Jima so important to the United States' war strategy?

    a) It was the only place in the Pacific to find fresh water for the Navy ships.

    b) It had airfields that could be used by damaged B-29 bombers to make emergency landings.

    c) It was the location of a secret Japanese palace that the Marines wanted to capture.

    d) Its volcanic ash could be used to make new uniforms for the Marines.

2. What was the main challenge the Marines faced immediately upon landing on the beaches of Iwo Jima?

    a) The beaches were covered in sticky, black volcanic ash that made movement very slow and difficult.

    b) The Japanese immediately launched a massive armored tank counterattack from the north.

    c) The ocean waves were too large for the landing crafts, sinking most of them.

    d) General Kuribayashi had disguised all his troops as palm trees.

3. What was the Japanese commander General Tadamichi Kuribayashi's main strategy for defending the island?

    a) He ordered all his troops to gather on the beach and launch immediate suicide charges.

    b) He surrendered early to save the lives of his 21,000 soldiers.

c) He built over eleven miles of crisscrossing underground tunnels and bunkers to fight from hidden positions.
d) He ordered all his men to retreat to the nearby island of Okinawa

4. What famous photograph, taken by Joe Rosenthal, became the ultimate symbol of American courage during the battle?

a) A picture of the B-29 bombers landing on the newly captured airfield.
b) A picture of General Kuribayashi surrendering to the American forces.
c) The picture of six Marines struggling together to raise a large American flag on Mount Suribachi.
d) The picture of a Marine commander yelling, "We aren't having any more wet oatmeal!"

1945
BATTLE OF OKINAWA

We're still in 1945, the final, fierce year of World War II. We've seen the Marines conquer the small, black-sand fortress of Iwo Jima. Now, the American forces were staring right at the next target: Okinawa (say it: Oh-kee-NAH-wah).

If you look at a map, Okinawa is not a tiny rock like Iwo Jima; it's a big island, about 60 miles long, and it sits just 340 miles from the main islands of Japan! Capturing Okinawa was the final, biggest, and most terrifying step before invading Japan itself. It was the last deadly leap the Americans had to make across the Pacific.

The stakes were incredibly high: The Americans needed Okinawa to use as a huge launchpad—a massive base for ships and planes—for the final invasion of Japan. But the Japanese knew this too. They decided to defend Okinawa with absolute determination, making it the toughest and longest battle of the entire Pacific War.

The Quiet Landing and the Hidden Trap

The invasion, codenamed Operation Iceberg (a good name, because the danger was hidden beneath the surface!), began on April 1, 1945.

The troops tasked with this giant invasion were a huge force: over 180,000 American soldiers and Marines. This was one of the largest forces the US had ever sent into a battle in the Pacific.

The landing was expected to be a catastrophe, just like Iwo Jima. But when the troops hit the beaches on the western side of Okinawa, they were met with... silence!

The Marines and soldiers walked ashore in disbelief. Where were the machine guns? Where were the snipers? It was an "easy" landing, which made every single soldier nervous. It was like going into a spooky dark house and finding the door wide open and a note that says, "Come on in!"

This peaceful landing was the Japanese commander's greatest trick. The Japanese commander, General Mitsuru Ushijima, was even smarter than the commander at Iwo Jima. He knew fighting on the beaches was useless. Instead, he pulled all his forces back and built his defenses in the rough, rocky hills of southern Okinawa.

He created a defensive line called the Shuri Line—an 8-mile-long fortress of underground caves, concrete pillboxes, and interlocking gun positions that ran straight across the narrow southern end of the island, ready to stop the Americans cold.

The Grinding Fight for the South

For the first two weeks, the Americans easily moved through the north and center of the island, capturing airfields and setting up their supply bases. It was almost too easy.

But when they turned south and ran straight into the Shuri Line, the war changed. The peaceful landing had been a massive setup.

The fighting that followed was called the "Typhoon of Steel" because of how intense the rain of bombs, shells, and bullets was on both sides. The battle quickly turned into a grinding, miserable slugfest:

The Terrain: Unlike the flat sand of the beaches, the south was all jagged, muddy hills, ridges, and hidden ravines. Every single hill was a fortress, and every yard of mud was covered by fire.

The Caves: Just like Iwo Jima, the Japanese were safe in deep, hidden caves. They would let the Americans get close, pop out to shoot, and then disappear back into the ground before they could be hit. It was incredibly frustrating for the American troops.

The American forces, used to quick "island hopping" victories, were now stalled. They had to use flamethrowers to burn out the cave entrances and heavy tanks to smash open the concrete defenses. Progress was measured in feet, not miles, and the battles for hills like Sugar Loaf Hill and Conical Hill were some of the most brutal of the entire war.

Historical Context: This battle was also unique because many local Okinawan civilians were caught in the middle of the fighting, tragically dying from both sides' fire as they hid in the same caves used by the Japanese soldiers. This made the fight even more complicated and heartbreaking.

The Kamikaze Horror

While the land battle was a nightmare of mud and blood, the air and sea battle around Okinawa was pure terror.

The Japanese Air Force launched their desperate, final weapon: the Kamikaze attacks.

A Kamikaze was a plane loaded with explosives and flown straight into an American ship. The word Kamikaze means "Divine Wind," and the pilots believed they were giving their lives to save Japan.

The ships supporting the land invasion—especially the destroyers, carriers, and supply ships—were hit relentlessly. It was a terrifying job to be a sailor off the coast of Okinawa. The Navy could only rely on their fantastic anti-aircraft guns and the brave fighter pilots in the air to shoot down the incoming Kamikaze planes.

Fun Fact! Did you know the Navy nicknamed the area around Okinawa "Typhoon of Steel" for the bombs flying, but they nicknamed the protective destroyer ships who stood guard closer to the island the "Picket Line"? Why?

...Because they were always picking out the enemy planes from the sky! (And, well, they stood straight like fence pickets!)

The American Navy lost 36 ships and had 368 ships damaged. It was the highest casualty rate the U.S. Navy suffered in a single battle during the entire war.

The Final Push

The battle dragged on for almost three months, from April 1st all the way to June 22, 1945. American forces eventually outmaneuvered the Japanese, slowly collapsing the Shuri Line and pushing the defenders to the very southern tip of the island.

The relentless ground assault, backed by massive artillery fire from the ships and air support, slowly crushed the determined Japanese defense. General Ushijima and his chief of staff were eventually cornered and committed ritual suicide in a cave overlooking the sea.

The American victory was complete, but it came at a terrible cost:

Over 12,500 Americans were killed.

Over 38,000 Americans were wounded.

On the Japanese side, almost every soldier died—over 100,000 troops. It was a victory, but a heavy one.

The End of the Pacific War

The Battle of Okinawa was the final, devastating battle of the Pacific War and, indeed, the final battle of World War II before the two atomic bombs were dropped on Japan shortly after.

What was the biggest lesson learned at Okinawa? It showed American leaders that if fighting for one tiny island was this bloody and long, an invasion of the main islands of Japan would cost hundreds of thousands of American lives.

Okinawa truly was the "Last Deadly Leap." The victory gave the Americans the final huge staging base they needed, and it forced the leaders to find a different way to end the war without a massive land invasion of Japan. It was the key to ending the war entirely, but the incredible courage of the soldiers, sailors, and Marines who fought there earned the island its tragic name: the Typhoon of Steel.

Quiz Time

1. **Why did the American forces code-name the invasion of Okinawa "Operation Iceberg"?**

   a) The weather was extremely cold, like a frozen iceberg.
   b) The American troops knew they would find a large ice cream factory there.
   c) It suggested that the most dangerous part of the defense was hidden beneath the surface.
   d) The island was shaped exactly like a block of ice floating in the ocean

2. **What was the name of the heavily fortified, 8-mile-long defensive system that the Japanese built in the rocky hills of southern Okinawa?**

   a) The Mt. Suribachi Line
   b) The Kamikaze Fortress
   c) The Shuri Line
   d) The Picket Line

3. **What was the terrifying weapon used by the Japanese Air Force against the American Navy ships during the battle?**

   a) B-29 Superfortress bombers loaded with nuclear weapons.
   b) Kamikaze planes (meaning "Divine Wind") flown straight into the ships.
   c) Giant underwater submarines disguised as whales.
   d) Floating mines that exploded when ships touched them.

4. **What heartbreaking lesson did the American leaders learn from the prolonged, costly fighting at Okinawa?**

   a) That the troops needed warmer clothes for the Pacific islands.
   b) That the American Navy was not as good at fighting as the Marine Corps.
   c) That the cost of invading the main islands of Japan directly would be too high in terms of lives lost.
   d) That they should have landed on the eastern side of the island instead of the western side.

1 Hiroshima Peace Memorial

1945
HIROSHIMA & NAGASAKI

We just survived the horrible "Typhoon of Steel" at the Battle of Okinawa. That battle, which ended in June 1945, taught the American and Allied leaders a terrifying lesson: the Japanese Army would fight with incredible determination for every single inch of land, right down to the last soldier.

After four years of fighting the huge battles of World War II, America was ready to go home. Everyone knew that an all-out, traditional invasion of the main islands of Japan—codenamed Operation Downfall—would be the bloodiest battle in human history.

The problem was huge: How do you get a determined enemy to surrender when they are prepared to fight to the death on their home soil?

President Harry S. Truman, who had only recently become President after Franklin D. Roosevelt passed away, faced the biggest, toughest decision any president has ever faced.

A Top-Secret Science Project

While the brave soldiers were fighting in the jungles of Guadalcanal and on the beaches of Normandy, a team of thousands of top scientists had been working for years on a secret project, known as the Manhattan Project.

This project was a massive, nationwide effort to build a weapon more powerful than anything the world had ever seen: an atomic bomb.

Imagine the difference between throwing a tiny pebble and throwing a giant asteroid! That's the difference between a normal bomb and an atomic bomb. The power came from splitting the tiny atoms inside materials like uranium and plutonium.

The science was incredible, but the goal was terrifyingly simple: create a single bomb powerful enough to make Japan surrender instantly, thereby saving the lives of the hundreds of thousands of American and Japanese soldiers and civilians who would die in a final invasion.

On July 16, 1945, the scientists tested their very first atomic bomb in the desert of New Mexico. The blast was so huge and bright that it felt like the sun had come down to Earth. The scientists knew immediately that they had succeeded, but they also knew they had unleashed a completely new kind of power.

Truman's Choice: The Hardest Decision

President Truman issued a final warning to Japan, called the Potsdam Declaration, on July 26, 1945, telling them to surrender immediately and completely, or face "prompt and utter destruction." Japan ignored the warning.

Faced with the projected casualties of Operation Downfall—which experts predicted would be between 500,000 and 1,000,000 Allied soldiers, not to mention millions of Japanese lives—President Truman made the impossible decision. He believed using the new weapon was the only path that could quickly end the war and, tragically, save the most lives in the long run.

Historical Context: This choice remains one of the most debated moments in history. Historians still argue about whether the bomb was truly necessary, but at the time, military leaders felt they were left with no other good choices.

August 6, 1945: Hiroshima

The mission began quickly. A specialized B-29 bomber, named the Enola Gay, took off with a special cargo: the first atomic bomb, nicknamed "Little Boy."

The target was the large industrial city of Hiroshima, a major military headquarters and industrial center in Japan. At 8:15 AM on August 6, 1945, the plane dropped the bomb.

The effects were instant and devastating. When the bomb exploded high above the city, it released an immense burst of heat, light, and pressure. A massive mushroom cloud rose miles into the sky. Within seconds, the center of the city was completely destroyed.

The blast immediately killed approximately 70,000 to 80,000 people and destroyed 90% of the city's buildings. The tragedy was immense. The power unleashed that day shocked everyone who heard about it.

After the bombing, President Truman again called on Japan to surrender.

Fun Fact: The pilot of the Enola Gay was Colonel Paul Tibbets. He had to fly incredibly fast away from the target after dropping the bomb so his plane wouldn't be destroyed by the shockwave! Talk about a speedy delivery!

August 9, 1945: Nagasaki

Japan's military leaders still refused to surrender, believing they could endure more. The American command decided they could not wait for the leaders to change their minds, as time was precious and more conventional fighting continued elsewhere.

Three days later, on August 9, 1945, the second atomic bomb, nicknamed "Fat Man," was dropped on the city of Nagasaki. Nagasaki was an important shipbuilding and industrial city.

Because of the steep hills around Nagasaki, the bomb's destruction was slightly more contained than at Hiroshima, but the resulting death toll and devastation were still horrible. Around 35,000 to 40,000 people were killed instantly.

The bombings of Hiroshima and Nagasaki, so close together, finally convinced the Japanese leaders that further resistance was completely futile. They realized the United States could continue to unleash this overwhelming, unstoppable power.

V-J Day: The War is Finally Over

Just six days after the Nagasaki bombing, on August 15, 1945, Japan announced its intention to surrender. This day became known as V-J Day (Victory over Japan Day).

The news of the surrender caused immediate, wild, and joyous celebrations all over the world. The long, brutal fight of World War II—which had begun in 1939 and had involved millions of people and thousands of battles—was finally, truly over.

The formal surrender ceremony took place on September 2, 1945, aboard the battleship USS Missouri in Tokyo Bay. General Douglas MacArthur, who had led so many of the battles in the Pacific, accepted the surrender from the Japanese representatives. The documents were signed, and the greatest war in human history was officially closed.

The New Age Begins

The bombings of Hiroshima and Nagasaki brought World War II to a swift and brutal close, undoubtedly saving the lives of the Allied soldiers who would have participated in the final invasion.

However, these events also opened up a whole new chapter for the world: the Atomic Age. The use of these terrible weapons led immediately to a desperate, decades-long competition between the United States and the Soviet Union to build bigger and better bombs, a period we now call the Cold War.

It taught the world that humans now had the power to destroy entire civilizations. This fact has forced countries to be much more careful about starting giant wars ever since. It was a dark, difficult ending, but it was the ending the world desperately needed.

Quiz Time!

1. **What was the top-secret science project that created the atomic bombs used on Japan?**

   a) Operation Downfall

   b) The Manhattan Project

   c) The Potsdam Declaration

   d) The Enola Gay Mission

2. **What was the main reason President Harry S. Truman decided to use the atomic bombs instead of launching a full-scale invasion of Japan (Operation Downfall)?**

   a) He wanted to test the new weapons as quickly as possible.

   b) He wanted to take revenge for the attack on Pearl Harbor.

   c) To save the estimated hundreds of thousands of American and Japanese lives that would be lost in a final invasion.

   d) He was told by military leaders that the bombs would only cause a small amount of damage.

3. **What were the nicknames of the two atomic bombs dropped on Hiroshima and Nagasaki?**

   a) Big Boy and Little Man

   b) Fat Boy and Slim Jim

c) Little Boy and Fat Man

d) Tiny Tim and Great Giant

4. What larger conflict or period in history immediately began after the use of the atomic bombs because of the power the United States now possessed?

a) The Space Race

b) The Great Depression

c) The Cold War (or the Atomic Age)

d) The World War I Rerun

1950
BATTLE OF INCHON

Welcome back, history adventurers! We've jumped forward five years, from the end of World War II, right into the middle of the Cold War! Remember how the world was divided between the United States and the Soviet Union? Well, in 1950, that tension boiled over in a small country called Korea.

North Korea, which was supported by the Soviet Union and China, suddenly invaded democratic South Korea. It was a complete surprise! The North Korean Army (KPA) was so strong and moved so fast that the American and South Korean troops—called the UN Forces (United Nations Forces)—were pushed almost entirely off the peninsula.

By August 1950, the UN Forces were squeezed into a small corner around the port city of Pusan. They dug in and fought desperately to defend this last bit of land, creating a defensive line known as the Pusan Perimeter. If Pusan fell, the war would be over, and the communists would win.

Joke Time: Why did the soldier guarding the Pusan Perimeter keep staring at his map?

...Because he was trying to figure out how to get a little more perimeter!

The UN Forces were running out of room, and they knew they couldn't just keep fighting backward. They needed a plan that was big, daring, and absolutely crazy!

General MacArthur's Big, Bold Bet

The commander of the UN Forces was a famous World War II hero, General Douglas MacArthur. MacArthur was a brilliant military thinker, but he was also known for taking huge, terrifying risks.

He had a wild idea: Instead of trying to punch their way out of the tiny Pusan Perimeter, they would land a giant invasion force deep behind the enemy's lines!

His target was Inchon, a port city on the west coast of Korea, close to the South Korean capital of Seoul.

The idea was almost impossible, which is exactly why MacArthur wanted to do it! He knew the North Koreans would never expect an attack there, because Inchon had three massive problems:

Monster Tides: Inchon has some of the biggest tidal changes in the world. The water level goes up and down by over 30 feet! When the tide is low, it leaves miles of thick, sticky mud flats where troops and landing craft would instantly get stuck. Landing had to be perfectly timed to a few hours of high tide.

The Sea Wall: The city was protected by a tall, steep seawall that soldiers would have to climb.

Narrow Channel: The path through the mud flats and channels to the city was long, winding, and easily defended.

When MacArthur told his own Navy commanders the plan, they were horrified! They tried to talk him out of it, calling it a "5,000-to-1 gamble."

MacArthur simply replied, "The history of war proves that the greatest difficulties... often lead to the greatest victories." He told them the enemy would never expect it because it was impossible!

The Perfect Day: September 15, 1950

MacArthur ignored all the warnings and pushed forward. The entire invasion was scheduled for one precise date: September 15, 1950, the one day with the perfect sequence of tides. If they missed that day, they would have to wait an entire month!

The invasion force, called X Corps, was huge: over 70,000 troops, mostly made up of US Marines, carried on 230 ships.

Phase One: Red Beach and Green Beach (Tidal Terror!)

Before the main attack, a small force landed at Green Beach (on a nearby island) to take out an enemy observation post. This was done quickly and quietly.

The main drama came later that day at Red Beach. At high tide, the landing ships charged toward the city. The Marines were instantly confronted with the steep, concrete seawall. They used ladders (just like giant step stools, but for fighting!) to climb up and over.

The North Korean defenders were completely shocked. They simply hadn't believed anyone would try to land at Inchon. The Marines quickly secured the port and began pushing inland.

Joke Time: Why did the Marines at Inchon refuse to eat pancakes?

...Because they had enough trouble crossing the mud flats!

Phase Two: Blue Beach and the Drive to Seoul

The next day, more forces poured onto the main beach (Blue Beach). The operation was a massive success!

The Marines and soldiers were now deep behind the North Korean front line. This was the equivalent of a football team running around the opposing team's defense and scoring a touchdown while everyone was still tackling at the line of scrimmage!

The War is Flipped Upside Down

The landing at Inchon had two huge, immediate effects:

The KPA is Cut Off: The main North Korean army, which was busy attacking the Pusan Perimeter, suddenly had its supply lines completely severed. They could no longer get food, fuel, or ammunition. They were trapped!

Breakout at Pusan: With the enemy distracted and cut off, the UN Forces holding the line at Pusan immediately launched a massive breakout offensive.

The trapped North Korean army was completely crushed between the two forces (Pusan in the south, Inchon in the west). The entire KPA was shattered.

Just days after the landing, the UN forces pushed into and recaptured the South Korean capital of Seoul. The city was liberated, and the North Korean invasion had been dramatically reversed!

The Cost of Victory

The Battle of Inchon was one of the most brilliant military maneuvers ever devised. It turned a looming defeat into a massive victory in just two weeks!

It boosted the morale of the UN forces and saved South Korea from being completely overrun. It proved that boldness and surprise could overcome almost impossible odds—and monster tides!

However, this victory also had a consequence. By crushing the North Korean Army, the UN Forces became confident and pushed too far north, right up to the border of China... and that's when things got truly cold!

Quiz Time!

1. **Who was the famous World War II hero and UN Commander who ignored all warnings and insisted on the risky landing at Inchon?**

   a) President Harry S. Truman

   b) General Douglas MacArthur

   c) General George S. Patton

   d) Colonel Paul Tibbets

2. **What were the biggest natural obstacles at Inchon that made the landing so difficult and earned it the nickname "5,000-to-1 gamble"?**

   a) Giant tidal waves that sank the ships at night.

   b) Miles of thick, sticky mud flats when the tide was low.

   c) Massive hills that blocked all visibility from the sea.

   d) Underwater volcanoes that could erupt at any moment.

3. **What was the primary strategic effect of the successful Inchon landing on the main North Korean Army (KPA) fighting at the Pusan Perimeter?**

   a) It forced the KPA to surrender immediately.

   b) It destroyed the KPA's entire fleet of tanks.

   c) It completely severed the KPA's supply lines, trapping them between the two UN forces.

d) It forced the UN Forces to push too far north toward China.

4. **What crucial city was recaptured by the UN Forces, just days after the invasion, symbolizing the dramatic reversal of the North Korean invasion?**

a) Pusan

b) B. Pyongyang

c) C. Seoul

d) D. Hiroshima

1950
BATTLE OF CHOSIN RESERVOIR

Last time, we saw General MacArthur pull off the impossible with the Inchon landing, pushing the North Korean Army (KPA) into a crushing retreat. With the enemy army shattered, American and UN Forces pushed north, aiming to end the war quickly and send everyone home by Christmas of 1950!

But the victory at Inchon led to a dangerous mistake: overconfidence. As the UN troops sped north, they crossed the imaginary line of the 38th Parallel and drove deep into North Korea, heading toward the Yalu River, which forms the border with China.

The Chinese government had warned the UN not to come too close to their border, but General MacArthur ignored them.

Joke Time: Why did the General ignore the warning signs at the Chinese border?

...He thought they were just telling him to have a "great wall of a time!" (Spoiler alert: It was not a great time!)

The UN forces quickly became spread out and separated in the rugged, freezing mountains of North Korea. This was exactly what the enemy wanted.

The Blizzard Surprise: China Intervenes

In late November 1950, near a remote, icy lake called the Chosin Reservoir, the weather was so brutally cold it felt like the freezer door was left open in the Arctic! Temperatures dropped to −35°F at night. Equipment froze, medicine turned to slush, and soldiers' frozen rations had to be thawed by holding them next to their bodies.

The soldiers were miserably cold. Why did the Marines at Chosin carry ice cubes?

...Because they were worried about forgetting what cold felt like!

But worse than the weather was the surprise! The massive, hidden Chinese Army—over 120,000 soldiers—had secretly crossed the border and surrounded about 30,000 American and UN troops, mostly the legendary U.S. 1st Marine Division.

In the darkness and freezing snow, the Chinese launched their massive attack. The UN troops were suddenly cut off, surrounded on all sides, and trapped by two terrifying enemies: the Chinese soldiers and the arctic cold.

Surrounded and Outnumbered

The Chinese Army had one simple goal: to completely destroy the US 1st Marine Division. The odds were stacked against the Marines: they were outnumbered by more than four-to-one, trapped in sub-zero temperatures, and surrounded by enemy forces who controlled the only escape route—a long, winding mountain road.

The situation was desperate. The Chinese constantly attacked, blowing up bridges and roads, turning the icy path into a deadly gauntlet.

The commanding officer of the Marines, Major General Oliver P. Smith, knew they could not stay put, but he refused to call the situation a "retreat." His famous quote became the rallying cry of the entire battle:

"Retreat, hell! We are merely attacking in a different direction!"

This was the spirit of the Marine Corps! They weren't running away; they were fighting their way out!

The Fighting Withdrawal

The Marines began what is known as a "fighting withdrawal." This was not a panicked run; it was a disciplined, slow, and ferocious fight down the mountain road. For 13 brutal days, from late November to mid-December, the Marines moved slowly, carrying their wounded and equipment with them, and fighting every inch of the way.

They battled through multiple Chinese ambush points:

Hellfire Pass: A section of the road where the Chinese had set up deadly traps, only for the Marines to blast their way through.

The Funchilin Pass: A key point where the Chinese had blown up a bridge. Since they couldn't drive their trucks across, U.S. Army engineers flew in huge, 2,900-pound bridge sections by parachute! This amazing feat allowed the convoy to keep moving. (It was the heaviest thing ever air-dropped by the military at that time!)

The Final Breakout

The goal of the withdrawal was to reach the port of Hŭngnam on the coast, where they could be evacuated by the Navy.

The Marines fought so fiercely that, even though they were outnumbered and surrounded, they inflicted devastating casualties on the Chinese. The Chinese Ninth Army Group was essentially destroyed in the battle, suffering such severe losses from combat and freezing that it couldn't fight again for several months.

When the Marines finally reached the port of Hŭngnam, the Navy was waiting. In what became known as the Hŭngnam Evacuation, over 100,000 UN soldiers, along with about 98,000 Korean refugees, were loaded onto ships and safely carried away to the south.

General Smith's "attack in a different direction" had worked! The Marines had not only survived an impossible situation but had done so while smashing the enemy forces sent to destroy them and rescuing thousands of civilians.

The Battle of Chosin Reservoir is remembered as one of the most heroic and difficult campaigns in American military history, proving that the strength of a soldier's will can be mightier than any army or any blizzard!

Quiz Time!

1. What major strategic mistake did the UN forces make that led to them being trapped at Chosin Reservoir?

- a) They ignored warnings about extreme weather and freezing temperatures.

- b) They crossed the 38th Parallel and pushed too close to the Chinese border.

- c) They failed to bring enough helicopters for the evacuation.

- d) They ignored the advice of their commanding officer, General MacArthur.

2. What was the main enemy the U.S. 1st Marine Division fought against at Chosin Reservoir?

- a) The North Korean Army (KPA) forces.

- b) The entire Soviet Army.

- c) A massive, hidden army of over 120,000 Chinese soldiers.

- d) A surprise force of Japanese holdouts from World War II.

3. What was the famous quote from Major General Oliver P. Smith regarding the Marine "retreat"?

- a) "We need to get home for Christmas, fast!"

- b) "The cold is our enemy now, abandon everything!"

c) "Retreat, hell! We are merely attacking in a different direction!"

d) "Wait for the Navy to come and rescue us here!"

4. **What extraordinary method did U.S. Army engineers use to repair the crucial blown-up bridge at the Funchilin Pass?**

a) They used super-glue and rope to hold the old bridge together.

b) They built a brand new bridge in one night using local timber.

c) They flew in massive, pre-made bridge sections by parachute.

d) They used their tanks as temporary bridges for the trucks to drive over.

1961
BAY OF PIGS

We've jumped forward to 1961. The world is in the middle of the Cold War, which was a time of tense rivalry—not hot battles—between the USA and the Soviet Union. Think of it like two siblings having a super intense staring contest: nobody wants to blink first, but they both spend all their energy just trying to look tougher!

Our story takes place just 90 miles off the coast of Florida, on a beautiful tropical island called Cuba. Now, a bay is a big curve of ocean that cuts into the land, and the "Bay of Pigs" (or Bahía de Cochinos in Spanish) is a famous one.

Joke Time: Why did the pigs want to open a history book?

...They heard they could find a bay full of their ancestors!

Before our story begins, Cuba had a new leader named Fidel Castro. He was a communist—meaning he was best friends with the Soviet Union (America's rival). Castro kicked out a lot of Americans who had businesses on the island and started turning Cuba into a socialist country.

American leaders, including the new young president, John F. Kennedy (JFK), were not happy about having a Soviet ally and a communist neighbor so close to the United States!

The Secret Plan: Operation Pluto

The US Central Intelligence Agency, or CIA (the government's super-secret spy group), came up with a bold, secret plan to get rid of Castro. It was a classic spy movie plot!

Here was the secret plan, which the CIA code-named Operation Pluto:

Find the Fighters: Gather up a group of Cuban people who didn't like Castro and had escaped to the US. These exiles were called Brigade 2506.

Secret Training: Train them secretly in Central America to be soldiers and fighters.

Surprise Attack: Help them sneak back into Cuba by landing at the Bay of Pigs.

Uprising! The CIA believed that when Brigade 2506 landed, the Cuban people would be so excited that they would drop everything, rush out of their homes, and join the invasion to overthrow Castro.

The plan sounded great on paper, but history shows that secret plans don't always work out!

President Kennedy's Big Decision

When President Kennedy first heard the plan, he was worried. It felt too risky. He had only been president for a few months and really didn't want the world to think the US was secretly trying to start a war. He worried if it failed, it would be a huge international embarrassment.

He was right to worry. The entire operation relied on one main thing: secrecy! If the operation wasn't a total surprise, it would be a total disaster.

Castro, however, was already a master spy himself! He knew the US was planning something. He was like a villain who saw the heroes' entire plan before the movie even started!

The Invasion Begins

The invasion started on April 17, 1961. Brigade 2506 finally landed on the beaches of the Bay of Pigs. They weren't met by cheering crowds ready to fight; they were met by Castro's well-prepared army!

The first problem was the coral reefs. The exiles had been told the bay had soft sand, but the bottom of the water was actually jagged rock and sharp coral! Their landing boats hit the reefs and got stuck, sinking equipment and making the landings slow and clumsy. It was like trying to sneak into a party but tripping over a giant pile of LEGOs!

The next problem was the air cover. President Kennedy had worried so much about being caught starting a war that he canceled several crucial American air support strikes. This meant when the Brigade's slow, stuck boats were attacked by Castro's Air Force, they had almost no air cover to fight back!

Total Disaster, Total Mix-Up

The battle lasted only three days before it became a total disaster.

The Cuban people did not rush out to join the invaders. Castro was more popular than the CIA had thought, and his secret police had already arrested anyone they suspected of helping the invasion.

The small force of about 1,400 Cuban exiles were heavily outnumbered by Castro's 20,000-strong military.

With their ships sunk and no air support, the invaders were trapped on the beach.

The battle ended quickly. Around 100 of the exile fighters were killed, and over 1,100 were captured and held as prisoners.

The Bay of Pigs Invasion was a huge failure for the United States. President Kennedy had tried to keep the US involvement secret, but everyone knew the US military had trained and supported the invaders. It looked like the young president didn't know what he was doing, and it made Castro look even stronger.

The Long-Lasting Consequences

Though a quick fight, the Bay of Pigs had huge, long-lasting consequences for the world:

It pushed Cuba and the Soviet Union even closer. Castro now completely distrusted the US and was desperate for stronger protection, which he soon asked the Soviet Union to provide.

It led directly to the Cuban Missile Crisis. Because Castro felt exposed, the Soviets agreed to place nuclear missiles in Cuba just a year later. This brought the US and the Soviets closer to a nuclear war than at any other time in history!

It embarrassed President Kennedy. He learned a painful lesson: never rely on a plan that requires everything to go perfectly right. He would later say, "Victory has a hundred fathers and defeat is an orphan." (Meaning, when you lose, no one wants to take the blame!)

The Bay of Pigs is a key battle in Cold War history, showing that sometimes, the biggest battles are won or lost not with tanks or soldiers, but by secret plans, bad intelligence, and the power of a giant surprise—even if the surprise is on the wrong side!

Quiz Time!

1. **The US Central Intelligence Agency (CIA) gave their secret plan to overthrow Fidel Castro a specific code name. What was that code name?**

   a) Operation Desert Storm

   b) Operation Cobra

   c) Operation Pluto

   d) Operation Overlord

2. **What was the major problem the Cuban exile fighters (Brigade 2506) ran into immediately upon landing at the Bay of Pigs?**

   a) They were attacked by sharks and crocodiles in the water

   b) Their landing boats got stuck and sank on unexpected jagged coral reefs

   c) They discovered that Fidel Castro had fled the country the day before

   d) The U.S. Navy mistakenly attacked their ships instead of the Cuban forces

3. **The invasion failed largely because President Kennedy cancelled which crucial part of the original plan?**

   a) The training of the exile fighters in Central America.

b) The delivery of food and water to the troops on the beach.

c) The crucial American air support strikes needed to fight Castro's Air Force.

d) The radio broadcast meant to encourage a civilian uprising.

4. **What long-lasting consequence resulted directly from the failure of the Bay of Pigs Invasion?**

a) The Soviet Union removed all military advisers from Cuba.

b) B. It embarrassed President Kennedy but convinced him to invade Cuba later.

c) C. It forced the U.S. to pay a large fine to Cuba for sinking their boats.

d) D. It strengthened Cuba's relationship with the Soviet Union, leading to the Cuban Missile Crisis a year later.

1965
BATTLE OF IA DRANG VALLEY

We're zooming forward in our time machine to 1965. The place is Vietnam, and the conflict here is heating up! Remember how the Cold War was like a giant staring contest between the USA and the Soviet Union? Well, sometimes, the rivals would choose two other countries to fight for them. These were called proxy wars, and Vietnam was the biggest one. The US wanted to stop Communism (supported by the Soviets) from taking over South Vietnam.

Before 1965, American troops were mostly just advisers to the South Vietnamese Army. But that year, everything changed. American forces were officially sent to Vietnam, and they were bringing something totally new to the fight: the helicopter!

Joke Time: What do you call a flying military horse?

...The Air Cavalry! (And yes, that's exactly what the US Army called their new air assault unit!)

This chapter is about the very first major battle between US ground troops and the North Vietnamese Army (NVA). It happened in a remote, wild, and dangerous place called the Ia Drang Valley.

The Valley of the Shadow

The Ia Drang Valley was a hidden, swampy area near the border of Cambodia. It was like the perfect hideout for the NVA—a secret highway where they could sneak soldiers and supplies into South Vietnam. It was tough terrain: thick jungles, sharp mountains, and tall grass that hid everything.

The American plan was to use their amazing new technology—the helicopter—to find these hidden enemy groups and fight them before they could attack South

Vietnamese cities. They wouldn't march in; they would fly in! This whole new way of fighting was called Air Cavalry or Air Assault.

In October 1965, the NVA attacked a US Special Forces camp near the Ia Drang Valley, and the American command decided it was time to hunt them down. The unit sent in was the 1st Battalion of the 7th Cavalry, commanded by Lieutenant Colonel Hal Moore.

Hal Moore was a brilliant leader. He knew this was the start of something huge, and he was determined to prove that the Air Cavalry could win. The soldiers in his unit were known for shouting, "Garry Owen!" This was a cheer left over from the days when the 7th Cavalry actually rode horses!

The Landing Zone: LZ X-Ray

On the morning of November 14, 1965, the first American troops choppered into a small clearing in the jungle near the Ia Drang river. They called this clearing a Landing Zone, or LZ. This particular LZ was named LZ X-Ray. It was shaped like the letter 'X' from the air.

Imagine this: The giant Huey helicopters roar in, stirring up huge clouds of red dust, and drop off groups of soldiers, four at a time. The moment the choppers lift off, the soldiers are alone, 100 miles from the nearest friendly base, and deep in what they knew was enemy territory.

Almost immediately, the soldiers started seeing signs of the enemy. Not just small groups, but hundreds of them. The NVA had been hiding deep in the jungle, preparing to move, and the Americans had landed right on top of their main camp!

The Fight for LZ X-Ray

The battle was instant and ferocious. The NVA commanders were skilled and quickly launched massive waves of attacks, trying to overrun the landing zone before more American helicopters could arrive with backup.

The fighting was terrifyingly close-quarters—sometimes just a few feet away! The NVA's strategy was simple: get so close to the Americans that the US troops couldn't call in their devastating air strikes or artillery support without risking hitting their own men. This was called "hugging the belt."

Joke Time: Why did the NVA commander bring a ladder to the fight?

...Because he wanted to climb up and hug the American belt! (It's a scary tactic, but the soldiers had to be quick to use their speed and firepower!)

Colonel Moore's challenge was to keep his small, surrounded force from being completely destroyed. Every few minutes, he'd desperately call for more helicopters to bring in ammunition, carry out the wounded, and drop off just a few more soldiers. The battle raged for three days and nights. Soldiers used everything they had—rifles, machine guns, grenades, and sheer willpower. The Air Force pilots and artillery gunners fired as close as they dared, blasting the surrounding jungle and saving the troops repeatedly.

Finally, thanks to the heroic stand by the American troops and the incredible courage of the helicopter pilots who flew non-stop under heavy fire, the NVA attackers were eventually beaten back. The Americans had held the ground.

The Ambush at LZ Albany

The fight didn't end there. Soon after the main battle at LZ X-Ray, a different American battalion, the 2nd Battalion of the 7th Cavalry, moved to a nearby area. They were ordered to march through the jungle to another clearing, LZ Albany.

Unfortunately, this time the NVA was waiting for them! It was a deadly trap. The Americans walked right into a devastating ambush. NVA soldiers exploded out of the ground and trees, surrounding the American column and creating chaos.

The fighting at LZ Albany was even more disorganized and confused than X-Ray. The Americans were split up, out of communication, and caught in the thick jungle. For hours, isolated groups of US soldiers fought for survival, making heroic stands while waiting for rescue and assistance.

This phase of the battle was incredibly costly for the American side. But just like at X-Ray, eventually, American air support and the tenacious fighting spirit of the pinned-down soldiers were enough to beat back the NVA and break the ambush.

The Lessons Learned

After several days of fighting, the Americans left the Ia Drang Valley. This series of battles was a brutal and costly introduction to the Vietnam War. Both sides learned critical lessons that would shape the rest of the war:

What the Americans Learned (Lt. Col. Hal Moore):

Helicopters were essential: Air Cavalry worked! They could land troops anywhere, even in remote, unexpected places, and deliver supplies and immediate firepower.

Massive fire works: The combination of artillery, air support, and ground troops could overwhelm any enemy attack, no matter how large.

What the NVA Learned (The North Vietnamese):

Avoid US firepower: The NVA knew they could not win a head-to-head battle against American guns and planes out in the open.

Fight Close: The only way to win was to "hug the belt"—get so close to the Americans that the US couldn't use its superior artillery and air power. This kept the fighting personal and deadly.

The Battle of Ia Drang Valley in 1965 proved that the fight in Vietnam was going to be long, brutal, and fought by two enemies who now understood each other's strengths and weaknesses. The American ground war had officially begun!

Quiz Time!

1. What was the new military tactic used by the Americans, where troops were moved into the remote Ia Drang Valley almost entirely by helicopter?

　　a) Trench Warefare

　　b) Air Cavalry or Air Assault

　　c) Island hopping

　　d) Naval Blockade

2. What was the name of the first Landing Zone (LZ) where Lt. Col. Hal Moore's 7th Cavalry unit landed and became surrounded by North Vietnamese forces?

　　a) LZ Albany

　　b) B. LZ Huey

　　c) C. LZ X-Ray

　　d) D. LZ Garry Owen

3. The NVA used a tactic called "hugging the belt." What was the goal of this tactic?

　　a) To wrap around the American lines to surround them completely.

　　b) To get so close to the US troops that they couldn't call in their heavy artillery or air strikes.

　　c) To force the American soldiers to use only hand-to-hand combat.

d) To climb onto the Huey helicopters as they landed to sabotage them.

4. What major lesson did the NVA (North Vietnamese Army) learn from the Battle of Ia Drang that shaped the rest of the war?

a) That fighting the Americans required using more tanks and heavy weapons.
b) That the American Air Cavalry tactic was completely useless in the jungle.
c) That they should always retreat immediately after the first shot is fired.
d) That they should avoid fighting Americans in the open and always seek close-quarters combat to negate US firepower.

1967
OPERATION CEDAR FALLS

We're still in Vietnam, but we're moving from the remote jungle of Ia Drang to a place that sounds scary, but is actually shaped like a slice of pizza: the Iron Triangle!

The Iron Triangle was a small, forested area shaped like a wedge, located only about 25 miles northwest of Saigon (the capital of South Vietnam). Why was this small area so important? Because for years, the enemy—the Viet Cong

(VC)—used it as their main secret hideout and base of operations.

The Viet Cong were expert at hiding. The Iron Triangle was laced with miles and miles of underground tunnels that were often so tiny, American soldiers joked they must have been dug by gnomes! These tunnels held hospitals, weapons factories, sleeping quarters, and command centers. To the VC, the Iron Triangle was a hidden city; to the US forces, it was an angry, hidden hornet's nest right next to the capital.

Joke Time: Why did the Viet Cong soldier bring sunblock into the tunnels?

...Because he wanted to avoid a sun-tan! (They were underground all the time! Get it?)

By 1967, American commanders decided they couldn't just fight around this dangerous place anymore. They had to take it out. This called for the largest, most carefully planned operation of the entire war up to that point: Operation Cedar Falls.

The Grand Plan: A Huge Horseshoe

Operation Cedar Falls wasn't a battle to win one hill; it was a giant, two-week-long house-cleaning mission designed to flush out the enemy. The plan was so big it looked like a horseshoe trap on the map.

Imagine you have a giant toy box full of action figures (and maybe some sneaky pests). You want to shake the box and trap all the pests in one corner so you can easily scoop them out!

Here's how the American and South Vietnamese forces planned this "shake and scoop" operation:

The Hammer (The Landing): In the North, massive numbers of American Air Cavalry helicopters would land thousands of soldiers and gear, quickly forming a line—the straight edge of the horseshoe. Their job was to act as the "hammer," pushing everyone South.

The Anvil (The Blockade): In the South, two huge divisions of American and South Vietnamese troops formed a thick, immovable line—the curved part of the horseshoe, or the "anvil." Their job was to block the enemy's escape route toward Saigon.

The Sweep: The troops would then sweep through the Iron Triangle, pushing everything into the "anvil" where the enemy would be trapped and destroyed.

The Attack: Land, Air, and Fear

The operation kicked off in January 1967. The ground shook as 30,000 American and South Vietnamese soldiers moved into position. This was the largest concentration of ground troops the war had ever seen.

The paratroopers of the famous 173rd Airborne Brigade were some of the first to land. They jumped from giant transport planes called C-130s to secure the key roads and block escape routes. Helicopters roared non-stop, carrying in more troops, bulldozers, giant earth-moving equipment, and supplies.

The speed and scale of the attack caught the VC completely off guard. They had prepared for years to fight in small groups, running and hiding. They were not ready for a giant, organized military machine surrounding them all at once.

Joke Time: Why did the 173rd Airborne get kicked out of the school play?

...Because they were always dropping in unexpectedly! (Just like their surprise parachute landings!)

The Battle for the Tunnels

Once the troops were in place, the real challenge began: fighting the hidden enemy.

Since the enemy's main city was underground, the Americans needed specialists to find them. These brave soldiers were called Tunnel Rats. They were usually small-framed men, often from Australia or New Zealand, who volunteered to crawl alone into the pitch-black, narrow tunnels carrying only a pistol, a flashlight, and maybe a knife.

Imagine being a Tunnel Rat: The tunnels were incredibly tight, sometimes only two feet wide and four feet high. They were full of danger: snakes, scorpions, hidden traps called booby traps (like spears hidden beneath dirt floors), and enemy soldiers waiting in the dark. It was the scariest, closest-quarters fighting you can imagine, far worse than anything at Belleau Wood.

The "Tunnel Rats" were amazing heroes. They were like cave explorers, but instead of finding treasure, they were looking for weapon caches and intelligence. Sometimes they would find vast storage rooms filled with rice or equipment.

The American goal quickly shifted from destroying the enemy soldiers to destroying the enemy base. Giant bulldozers, called Rome Plows because they were capable of cutting down forests like the Romans of old, drove through the jungle, flattening the dense undergrowth. Engineers worked tirelessly to find and blast the tunnels closed.

Success or Surprise?

Operation Cedar Falls was successful in several ways:

Destruction of the Base: The American forces destroyed hundreds of tunnels, huge caches of rice (enough to feed 13,000 VC for a year!), and captured tons of weapons. They also located the Viet Cong's secret headquarters for the entire region and destroyed it.

Psychological Blow: The Viet Cong were shocked that the Americans had penetrated their greatest stronghold. They had always believed the Iron Triangle was safe.

However, the operation was also a learning experience for the Americans, with a surprising failure:

The Escapes: Despite the massive number of troops, the "horseshoe" trap didn't work perfectly. Most of the Viet Cong soldiers—the actual fighters—simply slipped away through the few remaining tunnels and escape routes that led to the nearby rivers or forests. The VC were masters of disguise and infiltration.

It was like setting a perfect mouse trap, but the mouse was already gone. When the American troops left after two weeks, many of the Viet Cong simply returned and began repairing the tunnels!

Historical Significance

Operation Cedar Falls, while successful at destroying the VC's stuff, showed American leaders a harsh reality: winning the war was going to be much harder than running a single large-scale military operation.

It demonstrated that the enemy was patient, hidden, and preferred guerrilla warfare over fighting big battles like Ia Drang. The fight wasn't just against men, but against the entire maze of tunnels and the hidden structure of the Viet Cong army.

The operation served as a strong warning to the Viet Cong, but unfortunately, it didn't stop them. The VC learned how to hide and move even better, preparing for an even bigger surprise attack that would hit all of South Vietnam a year later. But that's a story for a different chapter...

Quiz Time!

1. What was the main reason the Iron Triangle was so important to the Viet Cong (VC)?

   a) It had the only fresh water source in South Vietnam.
   b) It was where they stored their secret sunblock supply.
   c) It served as their main secret hideout with miles of underground tunnels for headquarters and hospitals.
   d) It had a clear, flat field perfect for fighting big battles.

2. What was the military goal of Operation Cedar Falls, known as the "horseshoe" trap?

   a) To run a giant, two-week-long operation to find and destroy the enemy's hidden base in the Iron Triangle.
   b) To set up a permanent US military amusement park near Saigon.
   c) To capture only the enemy's food supplies and rice caches.
   d) To win the war by capturing a single major city.

3. What was the nickname given to the brave soldiers who crawled alone into the small, dangerous underground tunnels to fight the hidden enemy?

   a) Rome Plows
   b) B. Sky Jumpers
   c) C. Paratroopers
   d) D. Tunnel Rats

4. **Despite destroying the Viet Cong's supplies and headquarters, what was the surprising failure or limitation of Operation Cedar Falls?**

a) The American Rome Plows broke down immediately.
b) Most of the Viet Cong soldiers simply slipped away through the tunnels and returned after the troops left.
c) The American commanders couldn't figure out where the tunnels were located.
d) The 173rd Airborne forgot their parachutes for the jump.

1972
EASTER OFFENSIVE

For our next adventure, we're zooming to Vietnam in 1972. At this point, lots of American ground troops had already packed up and gone home. The plan was called "Vietnamization"—which basically meant the South Vietnamese Army, called the ARVN (Army of the Republic of Vietnam), was doing most of the fighting, with the U.S. helping mostly from the air.

It felt like the war was winding down. Peace talks were happening in Paris (the French capital, not the one in Texas!), and everyone was hoping for a break.

But just like that moment when you think you've finished all your vegetables, and then Mom serves more broccoli, the enemy had a giant surprise waiting!

The North Vietnamese Army (NVA) decided to launch a huge, massive invasion. They chose to attack right around the Vietnamese New Year and the Easter holiday, which is why it's called the Easter Offensive!

Why did the NVA choose the rainy season for their big attack?

...Because they wanted to make sure they had plenty of mud-slinging action! (And the clouds made it hard for the US planes to fly!)

The Surprise Attack: Tanks Everywhere!

The North Vietnamese didn't mess around this time. Instead of sneaking in with tiny groups of Viet Cong in tunnels (like in Operation Cedar Falls), they launched a huge, old-fashioned, powerful invasion using armored divisions, just like in World War II!

Imagine a massive stream of metal monsters—hundreds of Soviet-made T-54 tanks—rumbling across the border, followed by huge numbers of foot soldiers. They attacked in three main places at once:

The North: Across the Demilitarized Zone (DMZ), the border between North and South Vietnam.

The Central Highlands: Aiming for the city of Kontum.

The South: Heading toward the key city of An Lộc.

The South Vietnamese Army (ARVN) was completely shocked. They hadn't seen this kind of direct, gigantic tank charge before. Entire ARVN divisions were quickly overrun or crumbled under the surprise and power of the NVA's new tanks and heavy artillery.

The City Under Siege: An Lộc

One of the most dramatic battles happened at An Lộc (pronounced "On Lock"). This was a city that stood between the invading NVA army and Saigon, the capital. If An Lộc fell, the NVA could drive straight to Saigon, and the war would be over!

The small ARVN forces inside An Lộc were immediately surrounded by thousands of NVA soldiers and heavy tanks. It was a terrifying siege that lasted over two months! The NVA pounded the city with artillery so hard that much of it was turned into dust and rubble.

Joke Time: Why did the General at An Lộc order everyone to eat soup?

...Because he wanted them to have enough artillery broth to go around! (Get it? Artillery barrage!)

The ARVN soldiers fought bravely, but they were almost out of food, water, and ammo. They were often fighting hand-to-hand in the smoking ruins.

America's Lifeline: Air Power

With most US ground troops gone, the responsibility to save An Lộc fell entirely to American air and naval power. This was a huge test of the "Vietnamization" plan!

American pilots flew almost non-stop, fighting through rain, fog, and heavy enemy anti-aircraft fire to bomb the NVA tanks and supply lines. This incredible air campaign was codenamed Operation Linebacker I.

Helicopters braved a constant storm of bullets just to drop food, water, and precious medical supplies to the desperate ARVN soldiers trapped in the city.

A-1 Skyraiders (big, propeller-driven planes nicknamed "Spads") and fast jet fighters swooped in, dropping bombs right on the NVA's trenches and tank columns.

The mighty B-52 Stratofortress bombers (huge planes that could fly very high) were called in. They dropped massive amounts of bombs from so high up that the ARVN soldiers on the ground couldn't see the planes, but they could feel the ground shake when the explosions hit the NVA positions, often just a few hundred yards away!

This non-stop air support—from tiny helicopters doing dangerous drops to the giant B-52s making the ground tremble—was the only thing that kept the ARVN defenders alive. The NVA just couldn't survive being constantly bombed from above.

The ARVN Holds the Line

After two brutal months, the NVA, having lost huge numbers of tanks and men to the powerful American air attacks, finally gave up their siege of An Lộc. They were pushed back, and the city was saved!

Similar defensive battles were won in the Central Highlands (at Kontum) and in the North (at Quảng Trị), though the fighting at Quảng Trị was a chaotic back-and-forth battle for months.

Historical Context and The End of the War

The Easter Offensive was a tactical defeat for the NVA. They lost over 100,000 soldiers and nearly all the tanks they had used in the invasion. The ARVN, with American air support, proved they could fight and win big defensive battles.

However, the war was still nearly over for the Americans. The US military had proven that air power was king, but they were tired of fighting a long war so far from home.

Later that year, when the North Vietnamese tried to stall the peace talks in Paris, President Richard Nixon launched Operation Linebacker II—a massive air campaign (often called the "Christmas Bombing") that targeted Hanoi and Haiphong. This shocking use of air power finally brought the North Vietnamese back to the negotiating table.

By 1973, the Paris Peace Accords were signed, and the remaining American troops left Vietnam. While America's direct involvement was over, the Easter Offensive remains one of the largest and fiercest demonstrations of combat power in the entire Vietnam War, proving that the helicopter and the bomber were the ultimate heroes when the ground troops had pulled out. The victory proved that the ARVN could fight, but it came with a warning: they couldn't survive without that powerful American air protection.

Quiz Time!

1. What was the American plan called that meant most US ground troops had already left Vietnam by 1972?

    a) Operation Linebacker
    b) Vietnamization
    c) The Tidal Wave
    d) Operation Cedar Falls

2. What made the Easter Offensive so different from previous attacks by the North Vietnamese Army (NVA)?

    a) They used only small boats instead of soldiers.
    b) They launched a huge, old-fashioned invasion using armored divisions and T-54 tanks.
    c) They dug the tunnels even deeper and hid all the fighting underground.
    d) They flew hundreds of jet planes to attack Saigon.

3. What was the name of the critical city under siege for two brutal months that, if it fell, would have allowed the NVA to drive straight to Saigon?

    a) Quảng Trị
    b) An Lộc
    c) Kontum
    d) Paris

4. What American military force was the "lifeline" that saved the South Vietnamese Army (ARVN) defenders at An Lộc and throughout the offensive?

a) Giant bulldozers called Rome Plows.
b) US ground troops sneaking back in through the jungle.
c) US Air Power, including helicopters, A-1 Skyraiders, and B-52 bombers.
d) US Marine Corps Tunnel Rats.

1991
BATTLE OF 73 EASTING

We're making a massive jump forward in time, past the Cold
War, to the very end of the 20th Century: the year 1991. Get
ready for a battle that was so fast, fierce, and high-tech, it was
over in less than a day!

We are in the middle of the Gulf War, also known as
Operation Desert Storm. This war started because a dictator

named Saddam Hussein from the country of Iraq decided to invade and steal the neighboring small country of Kuwait.

The United States led a huge team of countries, called the Coalition, to kick the Iraqi army out of Kuwait. After weeks of heavy bombing from the air (that was like the world's longest firework show!), it was time for the ground troops— the tanks and armored cars—to rush in.

The main job of the American forces was to drive deep into the deserts of Iraq and cut off the Iraqi Army's toughest fighting force: the Republican Guard. These were Saddam Hussein's most loyal and best-equipped soldiers.

Why did the Iraqi Army keep their supplies in the desert?

...Because they heard the Coalition forces wanted to give them a sand-wich! (But the US forces just wanted to stop their sneaky plans!)

The Invisible Enemy

The location of our battle is a completely flat, featureless desert in Southern Iraq. The battle is named simply after a line on a military map: 73 Easting. Think of it like a line on a giant treasure map!

In late February 1991, American armored forces, led by the 2nd Armored Cavalry Regiment (2nd ACR), were sweeping east across the desert. They moved so fast it was called the "Left Hook"—a surprise punch around the side of the main Iraqi defenses.

The problem? It was snowing—not snow, but a thick, pea-soup-thick sandstorm! It was so bad, you could barely see your hand in front of your face. This wasn't helping the tank crews.

But the Americans had a secret weapon that made them the world's best hide-and-seek champions: thermal sights.

Thermal Sights are like special cameras that see heat instead of light. Even through the heavy dust and sand, American tank crews could see the bright orange glow of Iraqi tanks and vehicles sitting still in the desert, waiting for an ambush! It was like cheating, but completely fair!

The Fastest Tank Battle Ever

The two sides smashed into each other in the gloom of the sandstorm on February 26, 1991.

The Americans were driving powerful M1 Abrams tanks. The Abrams was amazing for three reasons:

Fast and Powerful: It could race across the bumpy desert at high speeds.

Tough Armor: Its heavy armor meant that even if an Iraqi tank hit it, the shell often just bounced off!

Big Cannon: Its 120mm main gun was incredibly accurate and could destroy Iraqi tanks from miles away.

The Iraqis, mostly using older Soviet-made T-72 tanks, didn't stand a chance.

The American attack was simple and deadly:

The M1 Abrams tanks would fire the powerful main cannons, destroying the Iraqi tanks from far away.

The M2 Bradley Fighting Vehicles (which are like armored battle taxis) would follow, using their smaller cannons and TOW missiles to destroy armored troop carriers and enemy positions.

The 2nd ACR advanced in a straight line, smashing through the Iraqi defensive positions one after another. Iraqi commanders couldn't believe it. The Americans were fighting in a sandstorm and could see them clearly!

It was a true David-versus-Goliath battle (if David had a laser-guided cannon and thermal vision!). The battle moved so quickly that American forces often drove right over the Iraqi trenches, not even realizing they had passed a line of enemy soldiers until later!

A True Blitzkrieg

The Battle of 73 Easting showed the world that the American Army was the master of high-tech, fast-moving war. The entire Coalition ground campaign lasted only about 100 hours before Iraq surrendered. That's less than five days!

In just a few hours of fighting at 73 Easting, the Coalition forces destroyed hundreds of Iraqi tanks and armored vehicles.

The Americans proved that technology like GPS (which helped them navigate the empty desert) and thermal sights (which helped them see the enemy) made a huge difference.

The victory completely shattered the best of the Iraqi army, cutting off their ability to fight in Kuwait and guaranteeing the tiny country's liberation. It was a speedy, stunning victory that showed the power of the US military's advanced armor and training.

This was a victory not just for the soldiers, but for the brave people of Kuwait, who were finally free after months of occupation. It was a perfect ending to the fighting part of Operation Desert Storm!

Quiz Time!

1. **What was the primary American military operation name for the combat phase of the Gulf War, where the Battle of 73 Easting took place?**

    a) Operation Left Hook
    b) Operation Desert Shield
    c) Operation Desert Storm
    d) Operation Enduring Freedom

2. **What American technology allowed the tank crews to see the enemy clearly, even when they were fighting in a thick sandstorm?**

    a) Powerful floodlights attached to the front of the tanks.
    b) Advanced Radar Systems.
    c) Thermal Sights, which see heat instead of light.
    d) X-Ray Vision Helmets.

3. **What legendary American tank was known for its tough armor and powerful 120mm main gun in this battle?**

    a) The M2 Bradley Fighting Vehicle
    b) The T-72 Tank (used by the Iraqis)
    c) The M1 Abrams Tank
    d) The Sherman Tank

4. **What military feature did the name "73 Easting" originally refer to on a map of the featureless desert?**

    a) The speed of the tanks in miles per hour.
    b) A specific line of longitude (a vertical line) on the map.
    c) A secret code for the biggest oil field.

d) The final number of casualties on the American side.

1991
BATTLE OF KHAFJI

We just zipped through the high-speed tank derby at 73 Easting, which was part of the huge ground attack called Operation Desert Storm. But before that giant "Left Hook" of tanks slammed into Iraq, there was one surprise party the Iraqi army tried to throw for the American-led Coalition.

This was the Battle of Khafji in 1991.

The Big Picture: Remember, for weeks, the Coalition had been bombing Iraqi targets from the air—it was like a giant, noisy game of whack-a-mole! The Iraqi army was hidden in trenches, getting pounded by planes day and night.

The Surprise: The Iraqi dictator, Saddam Hussein, wanted to prove his army wasn't beaten yet. He planned a surprise attack! He ordered his forces to sneak across the border and capture a small Saudi Arabian coastal town called Khafji.

Khafji was the first time that Saddam's army left their trenches and tried to actually invade the ground defended by the Coalition. It was a risky, desperate move, and it was about to kick off the first real ground battle of the Gulf War!

Why did the Iraqi army think attacking a border town was a good idea?

...Because they thought the Coalition forces would be too busy eating dates to defend it! (But the Coalition was definitely ready for a fight!)

The Rainy Night Raid

The battle started on January 29, 1991. It was dark, cloudy, and rainy—perfect sneaky weather! Iraqi tanks and armored cars, covered in mud and sand, rolled across the flat desert border between Kuwait (which Iraq was still holding) and Saudi Arabia.

The first defenders they met were a small group of U.S. Marines and Saudi Arabian soldiers.

The goal for the Iraqi forces was simple: grab the city, hold it for a few days, and look tough on TV back home. They hoped to convince everyone that the bombing hadn't worked and their army was still fierce.

The problem for the Iraqis? They ran right into a brick wall of unexpected resistance, determination, and smart technology!

Marines in Action: A small team of U.S. Marines was doing observation work near the border. When the Iraqi tanks appeared out of the darkness, the Marines didn't run. They called for air support and used their small, but powerful, TOW missiles to start fighting back! Even tiny groups of Americans showed incredible courage by taking on massive columns of tanks, firing their missiles and then quickly moving before the enemy could fire back.

A City Grabbed: Because the Iraqi forces had so many tanks, they were able to push the small Saudi and American forces out of the town overnight. By dawn, the Iraqi flag was flying over the empty, oil-soaked streets of Khafji.

It looked like a victory for Saddam, but the Coalition was not going to let him hold this prize for long.

The Allied Response: Saudi Firepower!

The Coalition response was swift and powerful. The main effort to take Khafji back was led by our friends: the Saudi Arabian National Guard. They were supported by U.S. Marine Artillery, U.S. air support, and a tank company of American M1 Abrams tanks.

The battle to recapture the city was close-quarters and intense. The streets and buildings became a maze of fighting where tanks had to drive carefully to avoid ambushes.

The Saudis Fight Back: The Saudi troops proved they were fierce fighters, moving house-by-house to clear out the Iraqi soldiers who were hiding in buildings.

The Invisible Shield: Up above, the U.S. Air Force ruled the skies. Whenever Iraqi tanks tried to move out of the city to attack, they were instantly spotted and destroyed by planes. It was like having a giant, angry, invisible hornet watching the sky, ready to sting anyone who stepped outside!

A Disaster for the Invaders

The Iraqi attempt to hold Khafji quickly fell apart.

For starters, many Iraqi soldiers were just hungry and tired. They hadn't been told to prepare for this mission; they were just ordered to move. As soon as the fighting got tough and the Saudi counterattack began, hundreds of Iraqi soldiers gave up and became prisoners.

The Iraqi generals were so focused on showing off on the battlefield that they forgot a crucial rule: You need to supply your troops! The men inside Khafji ran out of food, fuel, and ammunition almost immediately.

In less than three days, the Coalition forces had won the town back completely.

The Iraqi army's attempt to invade Saudi Arabia was stopped dead.

The entire Iraqi tank unit that led the invasion was wiped out or captured.

The Saudi and American forces had shown the world that their training and cooperation were unbeatable.

The Big Lesson of Khafji

The Battle of Khafji was a relatively small fight compared to the big battles of World War II, but it had massive importance for the Gulf War.

A Test of Will: It was the first time Saddam Hussein's army met the Coalition on the ground, and they were utterly defeated. This victory gave huge confidence to the Coalition forces, especially the Saudi troops who led the charge.

The Final Green Light: After seeing how fast and effectively the Coalition could organize and fight back, the American leaders knew they were ready for the biggest part of the plan: the full ground invasion to liberate Kuwait.

The Battle of Khafji was a quick, decisive action that proved one thing: when you mess with a friendly neighbor, you get the whole neighborhood fighting back! It was a quick victory that showed Saddam Hussein that his plan was going to fail, and his army was no match for the Coalition's teamwork and technology.

This ends our look at the first ground battle of Operation Desert Storm!

Quiz Time!

1. What was the main reason Saddam Hussein ordered his Iraqi troops to attack and capture the Saudi Arabian border town of Khafji?

    a) To test the effectiveness of American M1 Abrams tanks in combat.

    b) To find a secret Coalition air base hidden inside the town.

    c) To prove that the Iraqi Army wasn't beaten by the air bombing campaign and look tough on TV.

    d) To cut off the Coalition's supply lines coming from the Persian Gulf.

2. Which country's ground forces led the main counterattack to successfully recapture the city of Khafji?

    a) U.S. Marines, backed by U.S. Army Rangers.

    b) The Saudi Arabian National Guard.

    c) Kuwaiti resistance fighters and their allies.

    d) British armored divisions from the "Left Hook."

3. What military asset was crucial in spotting and destroying Iraqi forces attempting to move out of Khafji during the battle?

    a) U.S. Army tank companies fighting house-to-house.

b) U.S. Marines using powerful TOW missiles from armored vehicles.

c) The Saudi Arabian National Guard's night-vision goggles.

d) U.S. Air Force planes ruling the skies and providing "The Invisible Shield."

4. What major lesson did the Coalition forces learn from the quick, decisive victory at Khafji?

a) That the main invasion should have been delayed for several more weeks.

b) That the Iraqi army was not prepared to fight aggressively and could be easily defeated on the ground.

c) That the Coalition should rely more on naval power than on air power.

d) That Saddam Hussein's troops were masters of close-quarters urban combat.

QUIZ ANSWERS

1918 -BATTLE OF BELLEAU WOOD

1. A

2. A

3. D

4. D

1941 – ATTACK ON PEARL HARBOR

1. B

2. C

3. B

4. B

1944 - BATTLE OF THE BULGE

1. B

2. C

3. A

4. B

1945 - BATTLE OF IWO JIMA

1. B

2. A

3. C

4. C

1945 - BATTLE OF OKINAWA

1. C

2. C

3. B

4. C

1945 – HIROSHIMA & NAGASAKI

1. B

2. C

3. C

4. C

1950 - BATTLE OF INCHON

1. B

2. B

3. C

4. C

1950 - BATTLE OF CHOSIN RESERVOIR

1. B

2. C

3. C

4. C

1961 – BAY OF PIGS

1. C

2. B

3. C

4. D

1965 - BATTLE OF IA DRANG VALLEY

1. B

2. C

3. B

4. D

1967 – OPERATION CEDAR FALLS

1. C

2. A

3. D

4. B

1972 – EASTER OFFENSIVE

1. B

2. B

3. B

4. C

1991 – BATTLE OF 73 EASTING

1. C

2. C

3. C

4. B

1991 – BATTLE OF KHAFJI

1. C

2. B

3. D

4. B

Check out these other Amazing Titles from Intel-Excellence!

History & FACTS!

S.T.E.M. Activity Books!

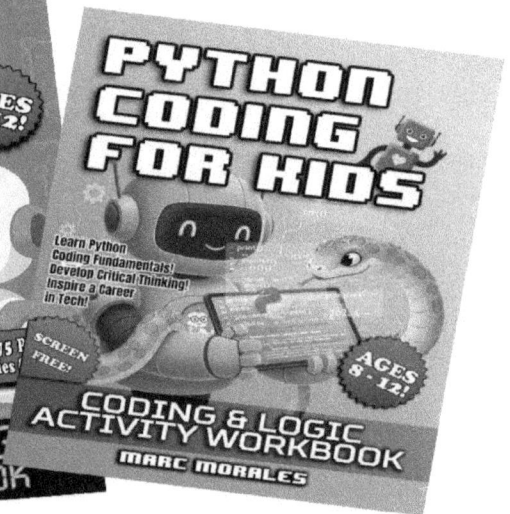

www.intel-excellence.com

About the Author

Ethan Carter

Ethan Carter is a forever student of World history and loves teaching and writing about history. He is a full-time staff of Intel-Excellence and works diligently on educating children and young people on U.S. & World History.

For more information please visit www.intel-excellence.com

.